FINANCE LEASING FACILITIES AND ITS IMPORTANCE TO SRI LANKA

Rashain Perera

The Copyright Act prohibits (subject to certain very limited exceptions) the making of copies of any copyright work or of a substantial part of such a work, including any unauthorized use, distributing, reproducing or similar process. The Publisher may be liable to criminal prosecution and civil claims for the damages caused. Written permission to make a copy or copies must therefore normally be obtained from the publisher (Nerdynaut.com) in advance. It is advisable also to consult the publisher if in any doubt as to the legality of any copying which is to be undertaken.

Copyright © 2018 Nerdynaut. All Rights Reserved.

Title: Finance Leasing Facilities and Its Importance to Sri Lanka
Publisher: Nerdynaut
Author: Rashain Perera
Edition: 1.0
ISBN: 9781973125747
Cover credit: Designed by Nerdynaut/Freepik.com

Table of Contents

1. EQUIPMENT LEASING AND ITS DEFINITIONS 1
2. ORIGIN OF LEASING FACILITIES 2
   - 2.1 IN THE GLOBAL CONTEXT 2
   - 2.2 IN THE SRI LANKAN CONTEXT 3
3. BASIC FEATURES OF LEASING FACILITIES 5
4. PARTIES INVOLVED IN A LEASING FACILITY 7
   - 4.1 LESSOR/ PROPERTY OWNER 7
   - 4.2 LESSEE 7
   - 4.3 VENDOR/ THIRD PARTY/ LEASING COMPANY 7
5. DIFFERENT TYPES OF LEASING ARRANGEMENTS 8
   - 5.1 FINANCE LEASE 8
   - 5.2 OPERATING LEASE 8
   - 5.3 DRY AND WET LEASE 9
   - 5.4 SALE AND LEASE-BACK 10
   - 5.5 LEVERAGED LEASE 10
   - 5.6 STEP-UP AND STEP-DOWN LEASE 10

6. LAW GOVERNING FINANCE LEASING FACILITIES IN SRI LANKA 11

    6.1 FINANCE LEASING ACT NO: 56 OF 2000 11

7. LEASING TERMINOLOGIES 12

8. DIFFERENT TYPES OF LEASE RENTALS 13

    8.1 ADVANCE RENTAL 13

    8.2 FIXED RENTAL 13

    8.3 LUMP SUM RENTALS 13

    8.4 BALLOON RENTALS 14

9. LEASE RENTAL CALCULATION 14

    9.1 MATHEMATICAL FORMULAE 14

    9.2 COMPUTER APPLICATIONS IN LEASE CALCULATIONS 15

    9.3 EXAMPLE CALCULATIONS 15

        9.3.1 EXAMPLE 01 15

        9.3.2 EXAMPLE 02: WITH ADVANCE PAYMENT 15

10. LEASE FACILITIES AND KEY CONSIDERATIONS 17

    10.1 CUSTOMER ELIGIBILITY 17

    10.2 SECURITIES AND COLLATERAL 17

10.3 APPRAISAL METHEDOLOGIES 17

10.4 STEP BY STEP LENDING PROCESS 18

10.5 DOCUMENTS IN LEASE FACILITY 18

10.6 REPAYMENTS 18

10.7 ACCOUNTING ENTRIES 19

    10.7.1 To record the inception of the lease 19

    10.7.2 To record the payments of lease 19

10.8 FOLLOW-UP AND SUPERVISION 19

10.9 DEFAULTS AND RECOVERY ACTION 19

11. LEASING VS LOAN FACILITIES 21

12. FINANCE LEASE VS HIRE-PURCHASE FACILITIES 22

13. INSTITUTIONS PROVIDING LEASE FACILITIES IN SRI LANKA 24

14. SIGNIFICANCE OF LEASING FACILITIES FOR SRI LANKA 26

REFERENCES 28

1. EQUIPMENT LEASING AND ITS DEFINITIONS

Equipment leasing is an agreement whereby the equipment owner transfers the authority to the lessee to use the equipment in return for lease payments agreed upon the lease agreements for a particular period of time conditions attached (Nevitt & Fabozzi, 2000). The provider of the equipment or the owner of the equipment is the lessor and the equipment user is the lessee (Nevitt & Fabozzi, 2000). Equipment leasing is very popular among businesses, especially where the production is capital based and is mostly favoured by small and medium scale businesses where high investment is needed if they were to buy on an outright purchase (Nevitt & Fabozzi, 2000).

2. ORIGIN OF LEASING FACILITIES

2.1 IN THE GLOBAL CONTEXT

The concept of leasing goes back to 2010 BC where agricultural tools were given to the farmers by the priests who were in effect the government officials in a typical lease agreement format (Miller & Upton, 1976). The concept of leasing developed rapidly with time and advanced with the ultimate objective of boosting the industrial sector following the industrial revolution and the movement from capital intensive strategies from labor intensive mechanisms. Leasing was used to finance properties in the past where it then developed to equipment leasing, housing, motor vehicles and ultimately for business purposes over time (Grenadier, 1996). The leasing system and regulations are different from operating regions which are shaped according to the local legislations, finance, and capital markets (Miller & Upton, 1976). The leasing industry is highly competitive at present that is flooded with many leasing providing companies and the demand is growing with the increase in the competition within industries mainly into manufacturing and service.

More digital and automated approaches in leasing can be also seen within the industry at present that has improved the efficiencies of the industry (Miller & Upton, 1976).

2.2 IN THE SRI LANKAN CONTEXT

With the introduction of trade and economic liberalization policies in the year 1977, a rapid growth in the industrial sector, banking system, and financial system were seen. The large scale firms who had the power of raising sufficient capital to increase their productions, purchased equipment on an outright basis to expand the production that helped in the boost of the economy. However, many medium and small scale businesses were also operating within the market that did not have sufficient capital to increase production by investing in new facilities, equipment, production lines, human capital etc. Thus a clear need for financing options for those in need was highlighted within the economy that was hampering the growth of the country, where the government took steps to receive the support of the World Bank (Woost, 1997). In 1980 with the surveys carried out by the World Bank a clear need to develop the capital market of the country was identified where leasing business came into being. In 1980, the first joint venture project was carried out where high demand was received from particularly larger businesses (Atapattu, 2009). The leasing business came into popularity in less time. However, unlike in the global leasing market, Sri Lankans used leasing facilities mostly to finance their motor vehicle needs rather than the businesses. The market developed rapidly and finance companies were registered under the CBSL. Currently, as per reports of CBSL as at 31st December 2016, there are 45 Finance companies providing various kinds of leasing facilities within the country (CBSL Reports, 2016/17).

3. BASIC FEATURES OF LEASING FACILITIES

The features of different leases can be different and following are the general rules or the general features of a leasing facility or agreement. However, there are many rules and regulations attached to a leasing agreement depending on the type of the lease which should be also noted in this regard.

- The lessor transfers something of value to the lessee on the agreement of value, time period and costs on both party agreement provisions to the laws and regulations.
- The subject of the lease agreement should have a value and the use of it should be significant and clearly stated in the lease agreement.
- The lease period should be clearly determined in the agreement.
- The lessee is liable for any damage caused to the property in use during the agreed period resulting from damage, misuse or any other similar case.
- The asset specified in the lease agreement should not be used for any other purpose that is not specified in the agreement.
- The ownership transference may depend on the type of lease as agreed upon the agreement.

- The main parties involved in a lease agreement are the lessor, lessee, and the finance company also known as the vendor.
- All lease agreements should comply with the relevant acts, rules, regulations, and laws relating to the operational boundaries.

4. PARTIES INVOLVED IN A LEASING FACILITY

4.1 LESSOR/ PROPERTY OWNER

The lessor is any person who is authorized to perform the leasing activity as provided by the Leasing Act No: 56 of 2000 (CBSL Reports, 2016/17). In other words lessor is the person who is willing to transfer his asset to the lessee over the lease agreement.

4.2 LESSEE

Lessee is the person who is based on the lease agreement that obtains the right to utilize the asset. The lessee is also liable to pay the payments as agreed upon in the agreement.

4.3 VENDOR/ THIRD PARTY/ LEASING COMPANY

The vendor is the legal party that facilitate the lease agreements complying to the rules and regulations in compliance with the Leasing Act. In simple, the vendor is the finance provider to the lessee and is the intermediator that acts in between the lessor and the lessee ensuring the conditions in the agreement are met.

5. DIFFERENT TYPES OF LEASING ARRANGEMENTS

5.1 FINANCE LEASE

A finance lease is relatively long term and cannot be cancelled on agreement. Examples can include a purchase of a machinery, plant, building or a ship that is generally of a higher cost or value. In a finance lease the risks, rewards and the ownership is substantially transferred to the lessee (CBSL Reports, 2016/17).

5.2 OPERATING LEASE

An operating lease is a short term lease that can be canceled where the lessor is responsible for the maintenance, insurance and maintaining the operational level of the asset. An example would be a tourist renting out a car or a hotel room during his/ her stay. In an operating lease, the lessor does not transfer the risks, rewards and the ownership of the asset to the lessee. The lease period will be generally lower than the economic life and the lessor would also expect a residual value at the end of the lease period.

Table 1- Differences between Finance and Operating Lease

	Finance Lease	Operating Lease
Ownership of the asset	With the company	With the company
Residual value risk	Not Applicable	Taken by the leasing company
Responsibility of maintenance and repairs	Lessee	Leasing company is the contract is taken and if not the lessee
Time duration of the lease	Most of the economic life	Part of the economic life

5.3 DRY AND WET LEASE

The dry and the wet lease are the two main types of aircraft leases. In a wet lease agreement, the organization or the party that owns the property provides the aircraft as well as one or more crew members to the lessee. Further, maintenance and insurance costs are borne by the lessor or the company that owns the aircraft. A Dry lease is different to a wet lease, where the aircraft is transferred to the lessee without the crew. Under a wet lease agreement, the lessor has only the operational control and no possession of the aircraft occurs in a wet lease agreement which makes it an exception to a typical lease agreement.

5.4 SALE AND LEASE-BACK

This is a special kind of agreement where the user may sell the asset owned by him to the lessor and lease back it from him on agreement.

5.5 LEVERAGED LEASE

Under this specific type of lease agreement, the lessor puts some money required for the purchase of the asset where the rest is borrowed from the lender. The lender will be given a senior secured interest over the asset in concern and on the assignment of the lease and the lease payments. The lessee can make the payments directly to the lender as agreed on the lease arrangement.

5.6 STEP-UP AND STEP-DOWN LEASE

A step up lease agreement is a typical lease agreement where the specified rent payments increases at certain future dates as agreed upon in the agreements. Step down lease is the opposite of the step up lease where the rent payments decreases on agreed future dates.

6. LAW GOVERNING FINANCE LEASING FACILITIES IN SRI LANKA

6.1 FINANCE LEASING ACT NO: 56 OF 2000

The law governing the Finance leasing facilities in Sri Lanka is the Finance Leasing Act No: 56 of 2000 (CBSL Reports, 2016/17). The Law provides guidelines on finance leasing business, qualifications for registration, applications, and certificate of registrations, annual registration fees, operating Manuel along with operational details and guidelines, duties, rights, and responsibilities of the lessee, lessor, and details of supply agreements. The Law controls and manages the activities by being a regulating body in order to protect the interest of various parties involved with leasing agreements. The current Act is the 7th revision which was updated on 3rd December 2016 (CBSL Reports, 2016/17).

7. LEASING TERMINOLOGIES

- Active lease; a lease that has been activated and is in operation whose initial term has not expired as yet can be simply known as an active lease.
- Buyout; the transference or purchase of the assets by the lessee during the term or at the end of the agreed term on expiry of the lease agreement could be simply known as a buyout.
- Commencement date; the lease commencement date is the date at which the equipment under lease agreement is installed and in the operating condition up to the lessee's satisfaction as agreed upon the contract.
- Credit; the authority to obtain finances, materials or services on the promise of paying them at a defined future date.
- Fair market value; the price for the equipment or asset which is stated in the lease agreement that the purchaser would be willing to pay in the open market is the fair market value.
- Guarantor; the entity or the person that promises to perform all the lessee obligations.
- Guaranty; a promise that is generally written by one party to perform the duty is one party fails to do so upon agreement.
- Initial payment; can be referred to the first payment or the first installment as noted in the agreement.

8. DIFFERENT TYPES OF LEASE RENTALS

8.1 ADVANCE RENTAL

As advance rental is an advance payment concerning with an operating lease which is deducted from the amount of financing. For example if you are purchasing an asset on operational lease you may pay a particular amount as advance rent which will be deducted from the lease asset value and then paid on installment basis with the agreed rate of interest.

8.2 FIXED RENTAL

A fixed rental lease is a lease agreement in which the renter agrees to stay and pay the rent amounting for the period of time indicated in the agreement. For example the lessee may pay the lesser on agreed days with a specific amount where at the end of the time period the total would be equal to the lease amount plus the stipulated interest.

8.3 LUMP SUM RENTALS

Here a lump sum payment is paid as the rent of the lease agreement and this can be on the end day, an interim payment depending on the terms and conditions agreed upon the lease.

8.4 BALLOON RENTALS

Balloon rental is a lease rental payment that is made at the end of the lease period rather at the beginning of the period as down payment. Further balloon leases are those in which repayments are not made on a regular basis where they are made as funds become available in balloons.

9. LEASE RENTAL CALCULATION

9.1 MATHEMATICAL FORMULAE

Figure 1- Lease Rental Calculation and its formulae

$$Pmt = \frac{PV - \frac{FV}{(1+i)^N}}{\left[\frac{1 - \frac{1}{(1+i)^N}}{i}\right]}$$

Figure 2- Lease Rental Calculation and its formulae

$$PV = Pmt \left[\frac{1 - \frac{1}{(1+i)^N}}{i}\right] + \frac{FV}{(1+i)^N}$$

Figure 3- Lease Rental Calculations and Dealing with Advance Payments

$$PV - A \cdot Pmt = Pmt \left[\frac{1 - \frac{1}{(1+i)^{N-A}}}{i}\right] + \frac{FV}{(1+i)^N}$$

9.2 COMPUTER APPLICATIONS IN LEASE CALCULATIONS

With the advancement of technology many online and offline technology based platforms have been introduced to facilitate leasing calculations. Some of them includes online lease rental calculators, excel sheets, accounting packages for leasing such as Dell Business Lease, Leasit and many more.

9.3 EXAMPLE CALCULATIONS

9.3.1 EXAMPLE 01

Consider an equipment lease where the lease amount is 3500 with a residual value of 1000 and 4 monthly payments. The lease interest payment is at a rate of 9% and the monthly payment can be calculated as follows.

Figure 4- Example 01 Calculation

$$121.71 = \frac{3{,}500 - \frac{1{,}000}{(1+0.0075)^{24}}}{\left[\frac{1 - \frac{1}{(1+0.0075)^{24}}}{0.0075}\right]}$$

9.3.2 EXAMPLE 02: WITH ADVANCE PAYMENT

Consider an equipment lease with a value of 3500, where advance payments are due at signing, with a residual value of 1000 and 24 monthly payments. The lease interest rate is at 9% per year and the monthly payment/ rent can be calculated as follows.

Figure 5- Example 02 Calculation with Advance Payments

$$\text{Pmt} = \frac{3{,}500 - \dfrac{1{,}000}{(1+0.0075)^{24}}}{\left[\dfrac{1 - \dfrac{1}{(1+0.0075)^{24-3}}}{0.0075} + 3\right]} = 119.13$$

10. LEASE FACILITIES AND KEY CONSIDERATIONS

10.1 CUSTOMER ELIGIBILITY

Any party entering to the lease agreements should have the legal capacity to enter into contract as noted by the law and the Act relating to lease. All parties should agree on condition and faithful representation is a must or customer eligibility. Customer eligibility can differ based on the type of lease thus referring the guidelines before entering into lease agreements is essential.

10.2 SECURITIES AND COLLATERAL

Any property or asset that is kept as security of the payment and to ensure the authentication of the contract. A collateral is also a security of payment that is essential for the execution of the contract (CBSL Reports, 2016/17).

10.3 APPRAISAL METHEDOLOGIES

Different types of lease appraisal methodologies exist and some of them includes the billboard appraisal methodologies, income method of lease appraisals, capitalization approach etc.

10.4 STEP BY STEP LENDING PROCESS

Figure 6- Step by Step Lending Process

Organize your Documents | Get Qualified | Shop Loan Programs and Rates | Apply for a Loan | Obtain Loan Approval | Close the Loan

10.5 DOCUMENTS IN LEASE FACILITY

The documents related to leasing may differ according to the type of lease you are considering. Some of the general documents essential in leasing can be listed as follows (CBSL Reports, 2016/17).

- Leasing application
- Documents confirming the capacity of each party
- Lease application and rental applications
- Deeds of properties and collateral
- Valuation reports of properties that are certified by professional and charted valuators.
- Lease agreements signed and authorized by the parties

10.6 REPAYMENTS

Repayment simply refers to the installments, finance costs associated with the payback of the lease amount as agreed upon in the lease agreement.

10.7 ACCOUNTING ENTRIES

The accounting entries differ according to the lease type and the basic accounting entries can be presented as follows.

10.7.1 To record the inception of the lease

    Lease receivables Dr.

        Asset account Cr.

10.7.2 To record the payments of lease

    Cash Dr.

        Lease Receivable Cr.

        Interest Income Cr.

10.8 FOLLOW-UP AND SUPERVISION

Continued follow up is essential to ensure the repayments, to ascertain the asset condition and to ensure that all requirements in the lease agreement are met as specified. Finance companies are mostly on the duty of ensuring the follow up process.

10.9 DEFAULTS AND RECOVERY ACTION

The failure to carry out the legal binding as agreed upon the lease agreement could be simply known as the default. The innocent party has the right to show in from of the legal system or the law on default as agreed upon the conditions.

Any loopholes that will put the innocent party in loss on default payments should be considered at the time of agreement.

11. LEASING VS LOAN FACILITIES

Table 2- Finance Leasing Vs. Loan Facilities

Leasing Facilities	Loan facilities
A down payment is not necessary	Down payment is essential
The total of the asset value can be funded	Funding is only for a portion
Provision for maintenance and insurance	No provisions for maintenance and insurance
No ownership of the asset	Ownership of the asset
The risks are covered on agreement	No risk covered

12. FINANCE LEASE VS HIRE-PURCHASE FACILITIES

Table 3- Finance leasing Vs. Hire-purchasing Facilities

Finance lease	Hire-purchase facilities
The ownership is with the finance company or the lessor.	The ownership is transferred on the settlement of the final installment.
Lessor can claim the tax shield on depreciation.	The hirer can claim the depreciation tax shield.
The capitalization is done in the books of the lessor.	The capitalization is done in the books of hirer.
The full lease payments are eligible for the tax computation process in the books of the lessee.	The interest payments is the only eligibility for the tax computation process in the books of the hirer.
The main purpose of a finance lease is to use as a source of funding a high cost asset.	Hire-purchase agreements are usually used to finance relatively lower cost funding needs.

Finance lease does not require a payment as a down-payment.	A down-payment is required.
Under the leasing agreement, no option is provided to the lessee or the user to purchase the asset or the goods.	Hire purchase agreements provide the user with an option.

13. INSTITUTIONS PROVIDING LEASE FACILITIES IN SRI LANKA

As per Central Bank Information the registered finance companies of Sri Lanka as at 30th April 2017 are (CBSL Reports, 2016/17) Abans Finance, Alliance Finance, AMW Capital Leasing, Arpico Finance Co., Asia Asset Finance, Associated Motor Finance Co., Bimputh Finance, BRAC Lanka Finance, Central Finance, Central Investments & Finance, Citizen Development Business Finance, City Finance Corporation, Colombo Trust Finance, Commercial Credit & Finance, Commercial Leasing & Finance, ETI Finance, HNB Grameen Finance, Ideal Finance, Kanrich Finance, LB Finance, LOLC Finance, Melsta Regal Finance, Mercantile Investments & Finance, Merchant Bank of Sri Lanka & Finance, Multi Finance, Nation Lanka Finance, Orient Finance, People's Leasing and Finance, People's Merchant Finance, Richard Pieris Finance, Sarvodaya Development Finance, Senkadagala Finance, Serendib Finance, Singer Finance, Sinhaputhra Finance, Siyapatha Finance, Softlogic Finance, Summit Finance, Swarnamahal Finance, The Finance House, The Standard Credit Finance,

TKS Finance, Trade Finance & Investments, U B Finance and Vallibel Finance PLC (CBSL Reports, 2016/17).

14. SIGNIFICANCE OF LEASING FACILITIES FOR SRI LANKA

There can be wide range of reasons to convey the importance of leasing facilities for developing and under-developed countries like Sri Lanka. Some of them can be presented as below.

- Small and medium companies or organizations that lacks the legal personality and reporting requirements to raise finance through bank loans, capital markets and through equity financing can simply go for leasing facilities.
- Leasing facilities encourage and motivate and encourage the production aspects of especially small and medium enterprises which can be considered as the growth engine of the country.
- Higher flexibility is provided through leasing companies when compared with other financing options available for small and medium scale businesses.
- Investments and capital has been one of the major requirements to accelerate the growth and development of the country that should be facilitated by sufficient leasing facilities.

- Leasing can encourage competitiveness within the growing and emerging industries that will lead in the economic boost.

Thus it is clear that leasing is critical for a country like Sri Lanka where production aspects, investments, capital formation has been of major concern for the growth and development of the country. Leasing can encourage and accelerate the growth process of the country in simple.

REFERENCES

- Atapattu, A., 2009. State of microfinance in Sri Lanka. *Prepared for Institute of Microfinance, as part of the project on State of Microfinance in SAARC Countries.*
- CBSL Report References [Online]

    http://www.cbsl.gov.lk/pics_n_docs/09_lr/_docs/acts/fin_leasing_7th_rev.pdf

    http://www.cbsl.gov.lk/pics_n_docs/09_lr/_docs/directions/snbfi/snbfi_SLCsDirectionBook_Sep2011.pdf

    http://www.cbsl.gov.lk/htm/english/05_fss/popup/registered_fc.htm

- Grenadier, S.R., 1996. Leasing and credit risk. *Journal of Financial Economics*, *42*(3), pp.333-364.
- MH Miller, CW Upton
- Nevitt, P.K. and Fabozzi, F.J., 2000. *Equipment leasing* (Vol. 60). John Wiley & Sons.
- Woost, M.D., 1997. Alternative vocabularies of development? "Community" and "participation" in development discourse in Sri Lanka. *Discourses of development: Anthropological perspectives*, pp.229-254.

www.ingramcontent.com/pod-product-compliance
Lightning Source LLC
Chambersburg PA
CBHW031516210526
45464CB00007B/2941